Growing in Love

5

United, faithful, and life-giving

PRINCIPAL PROGRAM CONSULTANTS

James J. DeBoy, Jr., MA
Toinette M. Eugene, PhD
Rev. Richard C. Sparks, CSP, PhD

CONSULTANTS

Sr. Jude Fitzpatrick, CHM
Pedagogy

Rev. Mark A. Ressler
Theology

Rev. Douglas O. Wathier
Theology

Daniel J. Bohle, MD (Obstetrics and Gynecology) and Anne Bohle, RN
Family Medicine and Parenting

REVIEWERS

Sr. Connie Carrigan, SSND
Religion Coordinator
Archdiocese of Miami
Miami, Florida

Mark Ciesielski
Associate Director, Office of
Continuing Christian Education
Diocese of Galveston-Houston
Houston, Texas

Margaret Vale DeBoy
Teacher
Arbutus Middle School
Arbutus, Maryland

Diane Dougherty
Director of Children's and
Family Catechesis
Archdiocese of Atlanta
Atlanta, Georgia

Harry J. Dudley, D. Min.
Associate Executive Director
of Faith Formation
Archdiocese of Indianapolis
Indianapolis, Indiana

Steven M. Ellair
Diocesan Consultant for
Elementary Catechesis
Archdiocese of Los Angeles
Los Angeles, California

Kirk Gaddy
Principal
St. Katharine Campus/
Queen of Peace School
Baltimore, Maryland

Connie McGhee
Principal
Most Holy Trinity School
San Jose, California

Barbara Minczewski
Religion Formation
Coordinator
Diocese of Davenport
Davenport, Iowa

Sr. Judy O'Brien, IHM
Rockville Centre, New York

Kenneth E. Ortega
Consultant for Media and
Curriculum
Diocese of Joliet
Joliet, Illinois

Sr. Barbara Scully, SUSC
Assistant Director of Religious
Education
Archdiocese of Boston
Randolph, Massachusetts

Rev. John H. West, STD
Theological Consultant,
Department of Education
Archdiocese of Detroit
Rector, St. John's Center for
Youth and Families
Plymouth, Michigan

Harcourt Religion Publishers

Nihil Obstat
Rev. Richard L. Schaefer
Censor Deputatus

Imprimatur
✠ Most Rev. Jerome Hanus, OSB
Archbishop of Dubuque
January 28, 2000
Feast of Saint Thomas Aquinas, Patron of Chastity and of Students

The Ad Hoc Committee to Oversee the Use of the Catechism, National Conference of Catholic Bishops, has found this catechetical text, copyright 2001, to be in conformity with the *Catechism of the Catholic Church*.

The nihil obstat and imprimatur are official declarations that a book or pamphlet is free of doctrinal or moral error. No implication is contained herein that those who granted the nihil obstat and imprimatur agree with the contents, opinions, or statements expressed.

Our Mission
The primary mission of Harcourt Religion Publishers is to provide the Catholic markets with the highest quality catechetical print and media resources. The content of these resources reflects the best insights of current theology, methodology, and pedagogical research. These resources are practical and easy to use, designed to meet expressed market needs, and written to reflect the teachings of the Catholic Church.

Photography Credits
Bridgeman Art Library: *Christ in the House of Martha and Mary,* c.1654–56 by Jan Vermeer (1632-75), National Gallery of Scotland, Edinburgh, Scotland: 21; **Comstock:** 52, 59; **Gene Plaisted/The Crosiers:** 39, 46; **Digital Imaging Group:** 4, 6, 7, 8, 11, 12, 17, 19, 28, 33, 36, 44, 45, 54, 56; **FPG International:** Gary Buss: 33; Antony Nagelmann: 15; Diane Padys: 9; **Jack Holtel:** 27, 28, 35, 38, 30; **The Image Bank:** Stephen Wilkes: 57; **Index Stock Photography:** 56; **Annamae Kelly:** *Quilter's Dwelling,* Second Grand Prize, The Red Apple Quilters, Royal Oak, MI: 44, 51; **Masterfile:** Jim Craigmyle: 23; **Photo Edit:** Myrleen Ferguson: 14, 15, 49; Tony Freeman: 31; R. Hutchins: 14; Michael Newman: 24, 44; David Young-Wolff: 29; **The Stock Market:** Peter Beck: 17, 48; Gabe Palmer: 17; **Tony Stone Images:** Penny Gentieu: 4; Don Smetzer: 13; **Superstock:** 9, 17, 21, 27, 36, 40, 43; **Unicorn Stock:** Kathi Corder: 53; Andre Jenny: 21; **Washington National Cathedral:** 52; **Jim Whitmer Photography:** 16, 17, 25, 57; **W. P. Wittman:** 23

Cover
Photo by **Superstock**
Illustration by **Kathy Petrauskas**

Printed in the United States of America

ISBN 0-15-950667-0

10 9 8 7 6 5 4 3 2

Growing in Love

5

God our Father, thank you for making us equal in your eyes. Jesus, show us the goodness in each other. Holy Spirit, help us respect and care for your gift of life.

Respect for Life

In the beginning God created the earth and filled it with life. As part of that creation, God made man and woman, giving them special responsibilities in caring for one another and for all living things. Six billion women and men now live on the earth. Yet God made one, and only one, you. You are a unique part of God's plan of creation.

All life is a gift from God. The Bible tells us that humans were created in God's image. God is good. Because you were created by God and created to be like him, you are good, too. As Scripture says, you have been "wonderfully made" *(Psalm 139:14)*.

Some of the physical characteristics and personal qualities that make you special are inherited. Imagine yourself at a family gathering. You might see in yourself many family characteristics. You and your aunt may have similar curly black hair. The shape of your nose might appear in every generation of your father's family. A number of your relatives may be musically talented. If you are adopted, you bring new characteristics into your family.

Your personality is also influenced by heredity. You may have your mother's determination to complete a project. You may be outgoing like your grandfather. Even though your inherited qualities influence your life, they do not keep you from becoming your own person.

Respect for Self and Others

God always loves you and expects you to become the best person you can be. Developing **self-respect** is a way of seeing yourself as God sees you—as someone with value and goodness. Respecting yourself allows you to honor God's gift of life and to make the best of your strengths and weaknesses.

Other people are also part of God's creation; therefore, we are called to respect them, too. Jesus gave us a very simple guide for showing respect for others. He said, "Do to others whatever you would have them do to you" (*Matthew 7:12*).

Different

Catholics Believe

God created men and women with differences that complement each other. Though different, they are equal in God's eyes.

(See Catechism, #2333–2334.)

From the beginning God made men and women to be different from each other. "Male and female he created them" *(Genesis 1:27).*

It's not difficult to think of ways that the male and female **genders** are different. The most obvious difference between females and males is in their bodies. Men and women also may have different ways of showing their spiritual, emotional, and intellectual traits. Men and women enrich each other with their different and unique gifts. They are meant to share their gifts with one another.

But we are more than gender; God created each person as an individual. Therefore, we cannot **stereotype** people by saying that all men are one kind of person and all women are another kind.

· Caring
· Loving
· Emotional
· Thoughtful
· Smart

· Curious
· Spiritual
· Confident
· Strong
· Honest

but Equal

In God's eyes all people are equal in dignity. The differences between the genders do not indicate how good or how important each group is.

Picture your classmates or other friends. The girls and boys in that group may have different kinds and colors of eyes, hair, or skin, and their bodies may have different shapes. Some are better at sports than others; some are better at math; some are good at both. So how can everyone be equal?

To understand in what way we are equal, we need to see each other as God sees us, as his own children. We are created in his image, and he loves all of us equally, no matter what we look like or what our strengths or weaknesses are. In God's eyes men and women are equal in dignity.

God's Gift

Protecting and caring for human life is a responsibility that begins in the family.

Scripture Signpost

What are humans that you are mindful of them, mere mortals that you care for them? Yet you have made them little less than a god, crowned them with glory and honor.

(Psalm 8:5–6)

The creation stories in the Bible tell about God giving humans an important responsibility. That responsibility is to care for all creation. In God's plan we have a special responsibility to protect life and care for all living things.

Your care of creation begins with the care of yourself. You are God's special creation, a physical and spiritual being. You show appreciation for God's gift of your body when you do all you can to be healthy. It's important to eat a variety of healthful foods, to exercise, and to get plenty of sleep.

Your mind needs care, too. Asking questions, learning new things, reading, and working hard in school all help develop your mental abilities.

When you recognize and express your feelings in appropriate ways, you are taking care of your emotional being.

You choose to care for your spirit when you pray, celebrate the Eucharist and the other sacraments, and treat all people with respect.

Respect for Creation

All things on earth are in some way connected. Living things have a special kind of connection. From the tiniest ant to the tallest tree, all living things depend on one another for life. Our own lives depend on trees. They provide us with oxygen to breathe, food to eat, products to use, and a shady spot in which to sit. Trees depend on us for a good growing environment. God asks us to be stewards, or caretakers, of creation.

Human life is also interconnected. When we are young, we depend on our families for food, shelter, and support. As we grow up, we see others depending on us, too. When we respect and protect all living things, especially other people, we show respect for God's gift of life.

Stepping **Stones**

Seeing with God's Eyes

Differences among people are good things that make each child of God unique. You can develop the good habit of seeing others with fairness and without **prejudice.**

1. **Think of someone who is different from you in age, ability, gender, race, or religion.**

2. **Picture yourself putting on special glasses that show you only what is good in others.**

3. **Looking through these glasses, see what is good in the person you first noticed as different.**

Showing Respect

You choose life and what is good when you respect yourself and others. In each balloon, write a specific way you show respect for the person or group named there.

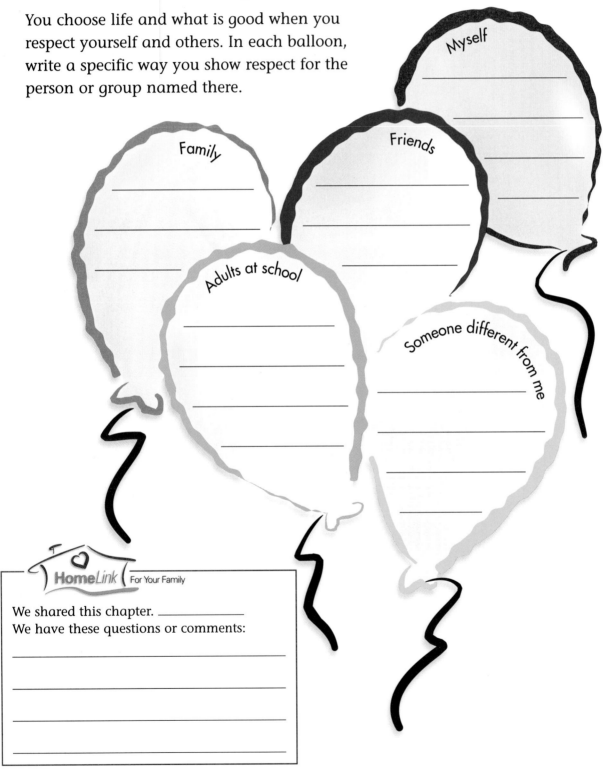

Myself

Family

Friends

Adults at school

Someone different from me

HomeLink For Your Family

We shared this chapter. _____
We have these questions or comments:

_____

_____

_____

_____

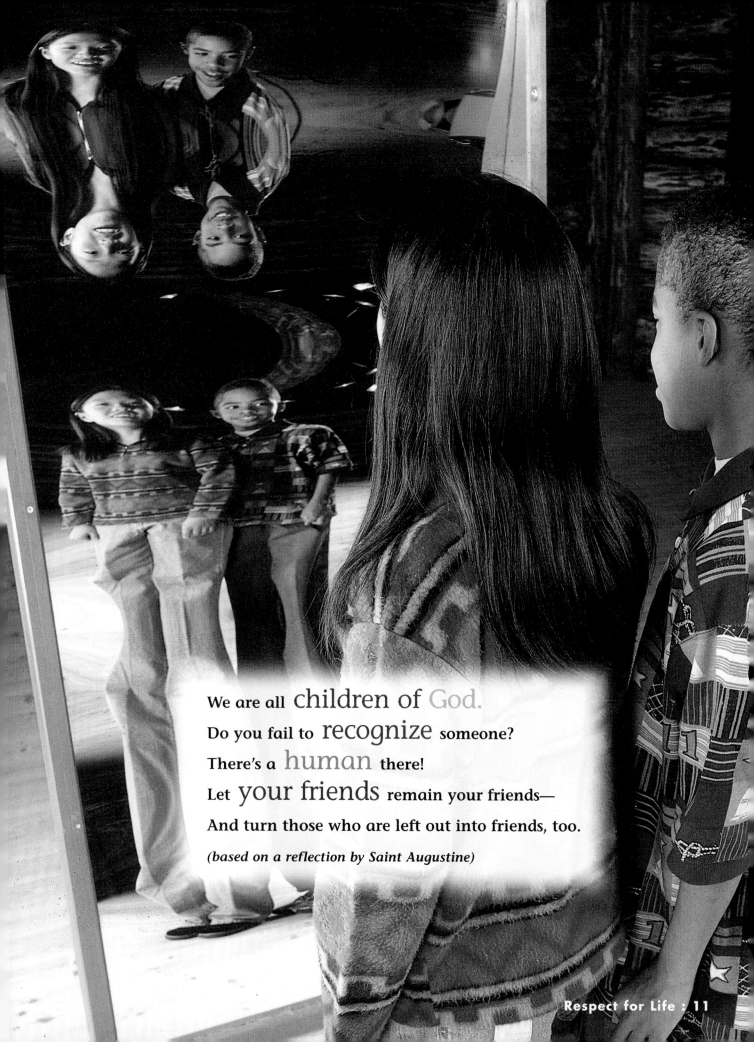

We are all children of God.
Do you fail to recognize someone?
There's a human there!
Let your friends remain your friends—
And turn those who are left out into friends, too.

(based on a reflection by Saint Augustine)

Chapter 2

God our Father, thank you for creating us as your children. Jesus, bless the people in our parish as they serve faithfully in their life's work. Holy Spirit, give us the wisdom we need to answer your call to love. Amen.

New Life in God

Baptism is a special, sacramental celebration. The blessed water, holy oil, lighted candle, and white garment used in the sacrament are reminders that God is present. Baptism establishes and celebrates our communion with the Father in Christ. Baptism is the beginning of new life lived in and with God, who is love, and the Church, which is the Body of Christ.

Called to Love

All people have a call and responsibility to love. Christians recognize that Baptism calls us to respond to God's love. There are many ways that Christians respond to God's call. Our lifelong journey offers us a variety of opportunities to live our **vocation** to love.

You have a special vocation. Your vocation is to be the best student you can be and to love as Jesus loved—to treat yourself and others with respect and dignity. When you do this, you help build up the Body of Christ.

Imagine that you're having a day when nothing is going your way. You're running late because your alarm didn't go off. You reach for your favorite cereal, but only a few crumbs are left in the box. When you finally arrive at school, you have to report to the principal's office because you're late. In class you discover that you did the wrong assignment. At recess a bigger student shoves you; his watch catches on your shirt and tears it.

How would you feel if these things happened to you? As a Christian who has a vocation to love, how would you respond?

Baptism calls us to live God's way of love every day. Think of one way you can do that today.

Witness Words

When did God's love for you begin? When God began. When did God begin? Never, for God is without beginning or end. So God has always loved you, through all eternity.

(Saint Francis de Sales)

Vocations

In their everyday lives adults respond to God's call to love by living a specific vocation. Each vocation reflects the same faithful, loving relationship that Jesus has with the Church.

Everyone is single for some time during his or her life. Some people are single only until they get married. A person who has been married may live as single again after a divorce or after the death of a spouse. Still others choose to remain single throughout life.

Single people may be more free to serve God and neighbor in some ways than married couples. For example, single people may have more time and freedom to do volunteer or missionary work or to take care of elderly parents or relatives.

Religious Life

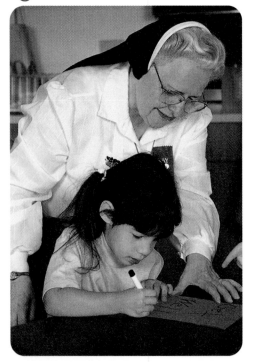

Single Life

The religious are single people who dedicate themselves in a special way to loving God faithfully by living a life of prayer or by serving the needs of his people. They belong to orders or communities in which they share their material possessions with other religious. Religious make public, sacred promises, or vows, to live in chastity, poverty, and obedience. Men religious are priests, brothers, friars, or monks; women religious are sisters or nuns. All religious live the vocation to love through their consecrated lives and their ministries.

Priesthood

Some men are called to ordained ministry as deacons, priests, or bishops. This vocation is celebrated in the Sacrament of Holy Orders, in which a man is consecrated and given a sacred power from Christ through the Church. In the sacrament the ordained man promises to faithfully serve as Christ's public servant. Ordained ministers dedicate their lives to serving God by serving God's people. Some priests are also members of religious orders, such as Benedictines or Jesuits. Priests preside at Eucharist and the other sacraments, preach the gospel, and lead the Church community. Most priests serve in parishes. Others work in hospitals or schools. Priests live and work wherever their bishops or religious community leaders assign them.

Married Life

God calls many people to the vocation of marriage. Through the Sacrament of Matrimony, God's grace is given to the couple to strengthen their love and unity. In the sacrament the bride and groom publicly vow to remain faithful and loving to each other for as long as they both live. A husband and wife take part in God's creative love in a special way when they help create, welcome, love, and educate children. They come to know God's unconditional love in the love they share with each other and with their children through daily experiences of sharing, caring, forgiving, and being forgiven. They express God's love in the everyday ways they help each other live holy lives and stay close to God.

Career Choices

We have come to know and to believe in the love God has for us. God is love, and whoever remains in love remains in God and God in him. We love because he first loved us.

(1 John 4:16, 19)

Whether adults are single, married, or committed to the priesthood or religious life, they still have **career** decisions to make. Within each vocation adults can do various kinds of work. For example, a single person may be a factory worker or a math teacher. A woman who is a religious sister may serve as a psychologist or teacher or dedicate herself to a life of prayer. Most priests serve in parishes, but some work as teachers or chaplains. Others give retreats or work primarily with those who are poor. Married couples may have separate jobs at home, in factories, in stores, or in offices, or they may work together in a family business.

Each career offers many ways to respond to God's love by showing love to others, especially those who feel unloved or forgotten. Jesus told us to love God above all else and love our neighbors as ourselves for the love of God. *(See Luke 10:27.)* As Christians we love others because we love God.

It may take some searching to discover how you can best respond in your life's work to God's call to love. But you can start with this basic truth: God created each of us to love and to be loved.

Showing Love

There are different kinds of love and ways to express love. Some kinds of love include married love, friendship, and the love between a parent and child. There is also the love for all people; that is, the desire for what is good for others. We can call this love unselfish because it expects nothing in return.

There are many ways to practice love. Do something every day to make life better for others. Treat each person with respect and justice. Be ready to forgive and to ask for forgiveness. Use words and actions that encourage the people around you. Remember others in your daily prayers.

Where are the places you are called to show love?

Challenge to Love

Imagine yourself as an adult with a special vocation and a career. In the space below, draw or glue a picture of what you see yourself doing in the future, either at work or with your friends or family members. Then answer the question.

How will you live a loving life? _____

_____

_____

HomeLink For Your Family

We shared this chapter. _____
We have these questions or comments:

_____

_____

_____

The time of business does not for me
differ from the time of prayer;
and in the noise and clutter of my kitchen,
while several persons are at the same time
calling for different things,
I possess God in as great tranquillity
as if I were upon my knees in prayer.

(Brother Lawrence)

Chapter 3

God our Father, we see your goodness in the relationships we form. Jesus, the Christ, we thank you for showing us how to love unselfishly. Holy Spirit, help us keep our lives in balance. Amen.

Life in Christ

Men and women are created unique. God gave people the gift of **sexuality** that helps them love and be loved. Human sexuality refers to what it means to be male or female. It is related to how people are formed—physically, spiritually, mentally, and emotionally. All of those aspects of sexuality together help people give and receive love.

A gift is a present that is given to show love or make another person happy. It is given freely, without expecting any kind of payment. Jesus showed us that all good relationships are based on love offered as a gift. This love is open and respectful.

When the crowds were hungry, Jesus fed them. After he heard of Lazarus's death, Jesus journeyed to Bethany to comfort his friends Mary and Martha and to raise their brother from the dead. When Jesus was near death, he prayed to his Father and asked forgiveness for those who were crucifying him.

Jesus reached out to those who were considered unlovable. He approached the lepers, who were shunned by others. He touched and healed sinners and those who were blind, deaf, or disabled. His heart was moved to compassion for those who were troubled and abandoned.

Jesus showed us how to be with others in ways that show love and respect.

Jesus treated all people with respect. When adults shooed the little children away, Jesus welcomed them and blessed them. At a dinner he forgave a repentant woman and allowed her to wash his feet, while the others didn't even want her in the room.

How do you show love and respect to your friends?

The way to live as Jesus did is to follow the guidance he gives us in John's Gospel: "Love one another as I love you" *(John 15:12)*. Loving others the way Jesus loves us is very challenging. It will take our whole lives to grow in this kind of love.

A Balancing Act

Gymnastics is a sport that requires timing and a great sense of balance. Picture a gymnast on a balance beam. Her mind is focused and the muscles of her body are controlled. Although she's been practicing for months, she keeps on practicing, knowing she can always get better. As her balance improves, she'll be able to add new maneuvers.

Regardless of their vocations, all adults balance several relationships at one time. Because relationships differ, the ways to give love may vary. What is proper behavior for one relationship may not be proper for another.

Chastity and Sexuality

Christians balance each of their relationships with the virtue of **chastity**. Chastity guides us in living our sexuality appropriately for our special vocations. It helps us exercise the control needed to keep the desires of the body and spirit in balance.

Sexuality includes your gender and affects all aspects of your person. It involves your feelings, the way you build relationships, and the way you express love. The virtue of chastity is the power that helps you enjoy God's gift of sexuality while respecting yourself and others. When love is given and received in a chaste way, no one is used or abused. The practice of chastity helps develop a love that can respond wisely and well to God and others.

Catholics Believe

Chastity integrates sexuality within the person. It guides the expression of one's sexuality in relationships.

(See Catechism, #2337.)

Balancing your body requires both mental and physical energy; balancing your life requires spiritual energy as well.

Adults sometimes have to work hard to keep their lives balanced, and so do you. You have to balance family, friends, school, and maybe a sport or other activity. To do this you need to develop good habits. The virtue of chastity also requires good habits that will help you handle all your relationships with care and respect.

What can you do at home this week to show love as Jesus did?

Chaste Choices

Scripture
Signpost

The fruit of the Spirit is love, joy, peace, patience, kindness, generosity, faithfulness, gentleness, self-control.

(Galatians 5:22–23)

You cannot expect to form faithful, chaste, and loving relationships as a teenager and as an adult just because you want to. Such relationships require time, attention, and effort. The relationships you have now are preparations for the long-lasting bonds you will form as an adult.

How to Be Chaste

Living the virtue of chastity requires the kind of regular effort that it takes to learn to dance or to play a sport or musical instrument. It takes practice to know and choose the appropriate behavior in a relationship. In a friendship between a boy and girl of your age, kissing would usually be inappropriate. Dating in general is not appropriate at this time. Social activities involving boys and girls in a group may be appropriate at times.

Self-control is a habit that puts you, not your impulses, in charge of your feelings, choices, and actions. It gives you the freedom to choose what is good for you and for others. Self-control is a habit that will help you make responsible decisions your whole life long. As humans we should have self-control; we should not be out of control or lose control of our own lives.

Self-control also helps you deal with pressures from other people and suggestions from the media. Pressure to engage in inappropriate sexual behavior can be overcome if you believe in your dignity and practice self-control.

Another dimension of chastity is modesty. You practice modesty when you show respect for yourself and others in the language you use, the programs and movies you watch, the magazines you read, the music you listen to, and the clothes you wear.

You can rely on Jesus to help you grow in love. When you become one with Jesus in the Eucharist, you receive strength to make choices and develop habits that show respect for yourself and for others. The weekly celebration of the Eucharist strengthens you to act modestly and chastely each day.

Everyday Chastity

On one side of the scale, label each weight with some pressure (such as TV) that could lead you to make choices that are not appropriate. On the other side, label each weight with a virtue or behavior that could help you deal with such pressures in a Christian way.

HomeLink For Your Family

We shared this chapter. _____
We have these questions or comments:

_____

_____

_____

May we grow in love
by the Eucharist we celebrate
in memory of the Lord Jesus,
who shows us the way.

(based on Prayer After Communion, #32)

Chapter 4

God our Father, we accept the responsibilities you give us as your children. Jesus, God's Son, thank you for helping us care for others. Holy Spirit, guide us to make choices that are wise and good. Amen.

Loving One Another

In the years following Jesus' death and resurrection, it was easy to identify his followers. Christians were recognized not by the type of clothing they wore nor by the part of town in which they lived, but by the way they treated people. "See how they love one another," people would say. The first Christians were filled with a love of God that sent them out to proclaim the gospel. They prayed, comforted those who were sick, and shared all that they owned so that no one was hungry or homeless.

A Commitment

We Christians continue to answer God's call to love by developing a sense of **commitment.** When we become members of the Body of Christ through Baptism, we become responsible for loving others as Christ did, regardless of race, nationality, or gender. We are part of a community in which members try to love one another wisely and well.

Commitment to a loving way of life involves time and effort, an unselfish attitude, and a determination to never give up. When you see a team playing hard even when it's losing or you watch a mother tenderly soothing her crying baby, you see commitment in action.

Our baptismal commitment calls for the same kind of self-giving, or **dedication.** As Christians we are to care for those who are hungry and thirsty and for those who are too young or too weak to care for themselves. We are to speak out for those who are treated unfairly, and we are to forgive and ask for forgiveness.

Today Christians throughout the world faithfully show their love by caring for others, especially those who are poor or are suffering.

Many of the activities we enjoy require us to make and keep commitments.

Building Responsibility

Christians have the personal responsibility to contribute to the good of others and to the community by educating their children and by working hard.

(See Catechism, #1914.)

Commitment involves responsibility. The word *responsibility* is related to the word *respond,* meaning "to answer." You are responsible, or answerable, for every choice you make. Being responsible means weighing your choices before you make them and looking for the choices that will result in the greatest good for you and for others. Before you make an important decision, you may want to consider some questions: Am I honestly trying to make a good choice? Am I deciding based only on what I feel like doing or on what is the right thing to do? Do I allow outside pressures to influence me to do something wrong? How will my choice affect others?

As members of the human family, we have a responsibility to care for one another.

Working together to raise money for a good cause is one way to exercise our responsibility to the community.

Responsible and Irresponsible Choices

When you were younger, you fulfilled your responsibilities by doing simple actions, such as brushing your teeth and putting away your toys. Now that you're older, your responsibilities are more challenging. Now they are often tied to more difficult choices, and being responsible means choosing what is right and healthy instead of what is wrong and harmful. Choices to smoke, drink alcohol, sniff poisonous products, or take drugs can lead to addictive habits that are harmful to our bodies and minds and are hard to break. Such decisions can have life-threatening consequences. Choosing to get involved in inappropriate relationships can place you in physical and moral danger.

As people mature and develop different kinds of relationships, their responsibilities expand to include others. But in some situations adults may feel out of control. They may hurt others with their words or even with violent actions. This kind of **abuse** is a sign of a serious problem that requires professional help. When such abuse happens, the person who is hurt is not at fault. If you know anyone in this kind of situation, it's your responsibility to tell a trusted adult who can get help for the person who is abused.

Scripture
Signpost

Watch carefully then how you live, not as foolish persons but as wise . . . Do not continue in ignorance, but try to understand what is the will of the Lord.

(Ephesians 5:15, 17)

Doing Your Part

Witness Words

Christ has no hands but your hands, no feet but your feet.

(Saint Teresa of Ávila)

Strange as it may seem, responsibility and freedom are connected. Being responsible means making good choices. When you're given responsibility, you are free to shape your own life by choosing what is good.

You are called to be responsible to yourself, and you fulfill this obligation by following your well-formed **conscience.** God's gift of conscience helps you know the difference between right and wrong and guides you to make good moral choices.

You also have a responsibility to love and respect your family. You do your part by treating your family members the way you want to be treated and by respecting your parents and older relatives. Asking "What can I do to help?" or "How was your day?" can be a good starting point because that shows you are thinking of more than just yourself.

Your friends count on you to be responsible, too. You can make them feel comfortable around you, show them you care about them, and be true to your word. You can also encourage friends to be the best persons they can be.

Even your community depends on you. At your age you may not be able to build a shelter for people who are homeless—but you can start a food drive, share food with a hungry friend, or welcome a new classmate.

Being responsible sometimes simply means doing what needs to be done and doing it willingly.

Stepping Stones

Working It Out

When friends disagree or argue, it's their responsibility to work things out. Use these ideas when you're involved in a disagreement. *Note: Take turns being the listener and the speaker.*

Listener

1. Look at the friend who is speaking.
2. Don't interrupt.
3. Try to repeat what you think you heard the speaker say.

Speaker

1. Look at the listener.
2. Use "I" sentences. ("I don't understand." or "I'm hurt by your words.")
3. Stay with whatever caused this problem. (Don't bring up what happened at other times.)

- Together, find two or three possible ways to end the disagreement.
- Without going against your conscience, look for a solution that lets you both have good feelings about the agreement. (This is called a "win-win solution.")
- Forgive each other.
- Remember, you can still be friends, even if you don't agree on everything.

Responsible Me

Print your name and age on the identification card. For each person or place listed, name at least one example of how you show responsibility by acting in a loving or just way. Put your picture in the space and your signature on the bottom line.

Name: _Daniela Marraoi_ Age: _____

Family: _____

Friend: _____

School: _____

Parish: _____

_____
(Signature)

HomeLink (For Your Family

We shared this chapter. _____
We have these questions or comments:

_____

_____

_____

Father of light,
send your Spirit into our lives
with the power of a mighty wind.
By the flame of your wisdom,
open our minds
and help us live in your peace.
(based on the Opening Prayer for Pentecost)

Chapter 5

God our Father, your life in us fills us with strength.
Jesus, be at our side as we face the challenges of
growing up. Holy Spirit, spirit of all that is good, lead us to
seek the guidance and forgiveness we need. Amen.

Led by Virtue

We know that we are "God's chosen ones, holy and beloved" *(Colossians 3:12)*. As Christians we believe that we are created in God's image and that we share in God's own life. We know that everything good is a gift and that we are God's beloved children. When we follow Jesus' example in our lives, we are practicing Christian morality.

Because of the first sin, original sin, we sometimes stray from the path of goodness and choose to turn away from God. As God's chosen ones we have been given free will, and we are often tempted to choose what seems appealing at the moment rather than what God wants. We are continually faced with moral choices, choices between what is right and what is wrong. Our choices affect our own lives and those of others.

Life is a journey. Sometimes you know exactly where you're heading, and sometimes you feel confused. The moral choices you make affect the direction of your journey.

Your **peers**, society, and the media may push you in a certain direction. They can **influence** the way you act and the choices you make. But you have the God-given power to evaluate their messages and make your own decisions.

It feels good to be accepted and liked by others. Your peers may urge you to experiment with language, dress, and different types of fun. These actions aren't bad unless they show disrespect for yourself or others or make you feel uncomfortable.

Some friends may urge you to smoke cigarettes, sniff glue, or do other things that are harmful to your body or mind. Or they may encourage you to do something that is against the law. At those times, remember that you can choose what is right and help your friends do the same. The best kind of friend helps you form good habits and choose wisely.

Society and the media are sources of all kinds of information, both good and bad. They are not always concerned with making you a good, moral person. They send you many messages, but you have to decide how to respond. You have the power to accept only the information that helps you lead a good life.

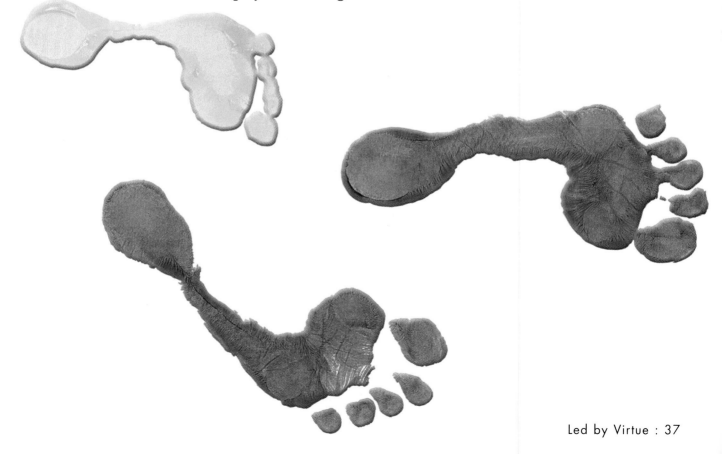

Making Moral Choices

Even though you have the power to choose what is right and good, you may still find it difficult at times. Making moral decisions is a challenge you will face throughout your life.

If you're ever lost, you know you can ask someone for directions, use a map, or call home. When you need help to head in a good moral direction, there are many places you can turn.

Begin with what God has given you. God's grace within you helps you resist temptation, avoid possible sin, and choose to do good.

Living a moral life involves staying away from evil, but it also requires moving toward good. God helps you do this by giving you **virtues**, or good habits. God's grace helps you practice virtues. Justice, love, temperance, prudence, and courage are virtues that make you a strong person who is confident about living rightly.

When you feel negative influences pulling you in the wrong direction, away from God, your well-formed conscience can be your steady guide. The forming of your conscience begins when you are young, and it continues throughout your life. Scripture, the teachings of the Church, and the advice of reliable guides help form your conscience so that you can choose wisely.

Scripture, God's word, teaches us about moral living. The laws to follow are clear. The Great Commandment to love summarizes all of God's laws. The Ten Commandments direct us to put God first and to think and act in ways that help us maintain a loving relationship with God and with each other. The Beatitudes tell us how to live as members of God's kingdom.

The Sacrament of Reconciliation reminds us how much God loves us and wants to help us live faithful, loving lives.

The teaching Church guides us through its statements on moral issues. The bishops in the United States have, for example, spoken out on racism, peace, and sexuality. Homilies often address ways to live morally in the light of the gospel.

Families, especially parents, are responsible for teaching children how to tell right from wrong, and you can learn from your family how to make these decisions. You can also find courage and strength in the examples of teachers, catechists, saints, and other faithful people you know.

God knows that people can be weak and that we sometimes do what is wrong. When we do wrong on purpose, we sin. When we are sorry for our sins, God forgives us. In the Sacrament of Reconciliation, we are forgiven, and we receive the grace to become stronger in choosing what is right.

Facing
the Challenges

Media messages send information to your brain in the form of electrical impulses. At times you may receive so much input that you feel like a computer with overloaded circuits. Whenever the messages go against what you've learned from your family and the Church, it's time to run a program that deletes these wrong messages and downloads the right ones.

In this case the "program" is in your God-given ability to think. Here are some guidelines:

- Limit the time you spend with the media so you can give your growing body the exercise, nutrition, and rest that it needs.
- Actively participate in life; listen to or watch media messages with a critical mind.
- Remember that each media message comes from someone's point of view. Some viewpoints don't reflect Christian values.

Television and Movies

Throughout history people have enjoyed and learned from stories. Today many of our stories come to us on TV or videotape. Some teach us the right way to live, but others do not. Stories about using other people in order to succeed may be entertaining, but they do not show Christian values. Stories that show someone making a sacrifice for the good of others can be just as entertaining and can motivate us to do the same.

Catholics
Believe

Moderation and discipline are important in evaluating the messages of the media.

(See Catechism, #2496.)

Mixed Messages

Which is the better source for learning about the gift of sexuality—people in the media, who don't know you, or people who do know and love you? Use these guidelines to evaluate media messages.

- **When you watch TV programs and movies, as often as possible do so with your family.**

- **Discuss with your family any of the messages about sexuality that go against what you know is right and good.**

- **Think about what you see and hear. What do the messages tell you about what it means to be male or female? What messages do you receive when you hear certain words or when characters dress in certain ways?**

Music and Electronic Media

Music media are designed to persuade people to buy videos, compact discs, or audiotapes. Those who create these products do all they can to make the music and the performers as appealing as possible. Because their primary emphasis is on selling their products, we can't always count on them to give us good, moral examples of how to look, dress, or talk, or how to love someone. Many times the producers of the media use sexual messages to make their products more appealing.

Electronic media, such as computer software and the Internet, can be entertaining and informative. Many people spend a lot of time using them. However, relationships can't be formed with machines, and you can't always tell which "information" is accurate.

Take a Good Look

Evaluate the story line of a television show or a movie for its moral messages.

What was the problem? _Someone wanted tomato_
Someone jelous
How was it solved? _She pretended to_
like someone she didn't.

Could it have been solved in any other way? _yes_
How? _She could have told him_
the truth.

_____

_____

Circle the words below that describe the characters' words or their treatment of each other.

kind   respectful   caring   angry
forgiving   (hurtful)   (dishonest)   loving

HomeLink | For Your Family

We shared this chapter. _____

We have these questions or comments:

_____

_____

_____

Where sin has scattered us,
may your love make us one again.
Where sin has weakened us,
may your power heal and strengthen.
Where sin has brought death,
may your Spirit raise us to new life.

(based on an Opening Prayer, Rite of Reconciliation)

Chapter 6

God our Father, thank you for calling us to love. Jesus, help us see in marriage the love you have for your Church. Holy Spirit, support all families as they live in faithfulness and openness to life. Amen.

Christian Marriage

A wedding is a special event. At the wedding ceremony and the party that follows, there are many signs of celebration. People wear special clothes. There are flowers and candles and rings. Family members and friends of all ages share a meal. The words of the readings, songs, and toasts all speak of love.

A wedding is more than a party. When a woman and a man enter into the **Sacrament of Matrimony**, their wedding celebrates not only the happiness of human love but also the holiness of human love.

Many preparations lead up to a wedding day. But this day is only the beginning of a lifelong sacramental celebration. The couple speak their vows before a priest or deacon and the gathered Christian community. Through this **exchange of consent**, the spouses promise to join their lives. They promise to live their vocation to love—as a faithful couple, as a new family, and as members of the Church.

The circular shape of a wedding ring is a symbol of unending love.

A Powerful Sign

Jesus was once a guest at a wedding in the town of Cana. When the wine for the wedding feast ran short, Jesus' mother asked him to help. Through his wonderful divine power, Jesus changed plain water into gallons of the best wine so the family wouldn't be embarrassed. *(See John 2:1–11.)*

This was Jesus' first public miracle. It wasn't only a favor for a friend. The miracle of Cana reminds us that marriage is also a powerful sign—a sacrament—of Christ's presence. Whenever we witness the joy of faithful love, family, and celebration, we see the future God promises us. That great future is made from the ordinary actions of our everyday lives, transformed by faith and the gift of God's grace.

Faithful

C a t h o l i c s
Believe

In Christian marriage the natural qualities of married love—lifelong fidelity and openness to new life—take on an even deeper meaning. These qualities are united in marriage, just as the husband and wife are united.

(See Catechism, #1643.)

The promises that a married couple consent to are signs of a covenant, a special, holy relationship. The covenant of marriage is like the covenant God made with the people of Israel—to be faithful and loving forever, through joys and difficulties. Like the covenant between Christ and the Church, Christian marriage includes not only love and care but also generosity, trust, loyalty, self-sacrifice, and forgiveness. All these qualities are summed up in the couple's vow of lifelong **fidelity.**

Some may think it's unrealistic to expect spouses to remain faithful to each other for life. Almost every other human contract has a built-in escape clause or a money-back guarantee. Unfortunately many people today look at marriage in the same way—as a temporary arrangement easily left behind at the first sign of difficulty. Through the Sacrament of Matrimony, the couple witnesses to us the depth of love and commitment humans are capable of.

Catholics believe that spouses can, with God's help, make and keep a lifelong vow of fidelity. They can remain in love for life. They can expect of each other a serious commitment to spiritual, emotional, and sexual faithfulness.

To celebrate their special bond of love, husbands and wives have the gift of the intimate expression of their sexuality called **sexual intercourse.** Within the covenant of marriage, sexual intercourse brings two people together physically, emotionally, and spiritually in the closest possible way. The pleasure the spouses experience in sharing this special joining of their bodies is intended to deepen their love and unity and demonstrate their willingness to welcome children.

Outside the permanent commitment of marriage, sexual intercourse cannot express its full meaning. Instead of promoting closeness and self-sacrifice, sexual intercourse outside of marriage can lead to selfishness and hurt. Separating the pleasure of sexual intercourse from a commitment to lifelong faithfulness and the possibility of children is wrong.

A married couple's sharing of faithful love includes more than sexual intercourse. The lifelong sexual relationship they share enriches and is enriched by all the other ways spouses grow in love together through difficulties and joys.

The Sacrament of Matrimony gives spouses the grace to love faithfully through the many stages of a family's life.

Open to Life

The love between a husband and wife has two dimensions. Love brings the couple together, and love calls them to be open to new life. Sexual intercourse expresses both these dimensions of married love. Through joining their bodies, a husband and wife experience a closeness that may also result in the **conception** of a child.

Through this wonderful gift God invites married persons to participate in his creative love. By opening their lives to children, a married couple expresses the **procreative** meaning of their love. Love is passed from generation to generation.

The gift of new life is precious. While parents are called to be responsible in conceiving children, the Catholic Church teaches that only natural means may be used to regulate conception. Other means, such as condoms and birth control pills, may not be used. When a marriage is not open to the possibility of new life, the love between the spouses may become self-centered, rather than generous and procreative.

A Lifelong Responsibility

Just as the wedding day is only the beginning of the lifelong journey of marriage, the conception of a child is only the beginning of parenthood. Spouses who become parents share in God's creative love throughout their children's lives. Becoming parents means making a commitment to care for a new life in every way—physically, mentally, emotionally, and spiritually. This great joy and awesome responsibility is supported by the grace of the sacraments, especially Matrimony, the Eucharist, and Reconciliation.

Sometimes it is not possible for married couples to conceive a child. The spouses are still capable of being life-giving in many ways. They may choose to adopt or become foster parents for one or more children. They may take on the responsibilities of mentoring children in their neighborhood or in a school or religion program. They may welcome into their home extended family members who are elderly or ill. By sharing in God's creative care for the gift of life, spouses make their love more generous and open. Their love for one another grows stronger the more it is shared with those in need of the love of a family.

Everyone Belongs to a Family

The call to share in God's life-giving love is not limited to married couples. Every person, no matter what his or her vocation or state of life, belongs to a family. Every person is capable of loving generously and of welcoming and caring for God's gift of new life. The special responsibility of conceiving children is intended for those who are married. But all of us are called to love generously in our relationships with family members, friends, and all others who touch our lives.

What are some ways your family is life-giving?

My Family Quilt

Use pictures, symbols, or words that describe your family to design this patch for a quilt.

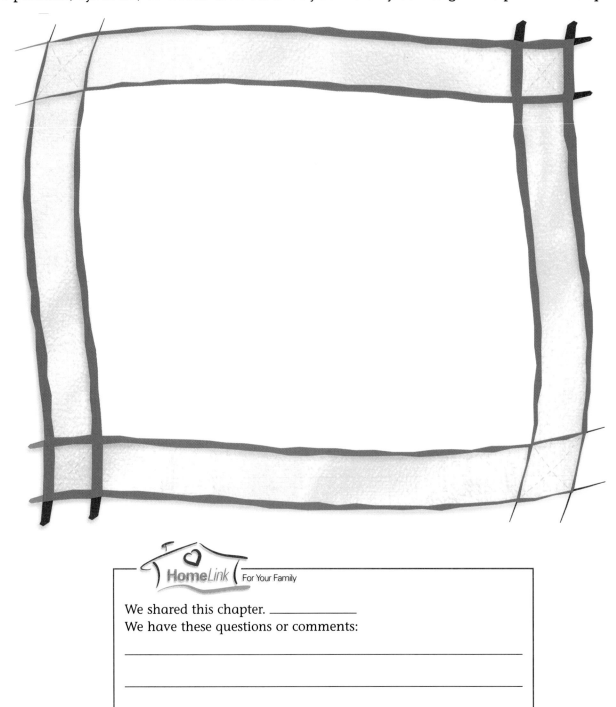

HomeLink For Your Family

We shared this chapter. _____
We have these questions or comments:

_____

_____

_____

_____

God the eternal Father keep you in love with each other,
so that the peace of Christ may stay with you
and be always in your home.

(from the Solemn Blessing, Rite of Marriage)

Chapter 7

God our Father, thank you for being with us in the people who love us. Jesus, God's Son, help us live our vocation to love. Holy Spirit, guide us in our prayer and action so that we may grow in love. Amen.

Living in Love

God is love, so wherever genuine love is, God is there. *(See 1 John 4:16.)* The Bible uses stories of human love to show God's love, which comes to us as forgiveness, trust, faithfulness, or loving care.

Where there is forgiveness, there is God.
A certain young man turned his back on his family. One day he asked his father for his inheritance and then went his own way. He spent the money foolishly and soon found himself living among pigs. With regret the young man returned to his father to ask his forgiveness. Without any anger the father ran out to meet and hug his son and celebrate his return. *(See Luke 15:11–24.)*

Where there is trust, there is God. Jairus went down on his knees and pleaded earnestly with Jesus to heal his dying daughter. Jesus saw Jairus's trust and brought the girl back to life. *(See Mark 5:22–24, 35–43.)*

Taking time to show our care for each other gives us opportunities to build loving, trusting relationships.

Where there is faithfulness, there is God.

When Ruth's husband died, she could have gone back to the country where she had been born. But she was concerned about her mother-in-law, Naomi, who would then be left alone. Ruth told Naomi that she would never abandon her. "Wherever you go, I will go," said Ruth. She was a comfort to Naomi in her old age. *(See Ruth 1.)*

Where a family shows care, there is God.

A story in the Bible tells us that when Jesus was a baby, an angel warned Joseph that their lives were in danger. During the dark of night, Joseph and Mary gathered their possessions and stole away to Egypt to protect and care for the child that had been entrusted to them. They stayed there until it was safe to return home. *(See Matthew 2:13–15.)*

Where there is love, there is God.

Being Together

People are meant to be together, and so they form friendships, deep relationships, and communities. One reason they come together is **attraction.**

The Role of Attraction

The messages in the media seem to say that attraction and love are the same thing. This is not true. Attraction is an urge or pull that draws people together. Even friendships are based on attraction.

At your age you are probably attracted to people of your own gender. This is normal and natural. In fact, throughout your life you will be attracted to and will want to form friendships with those of your own gender.

As our bodies develop and mature, most of us become attracted to people of the other gender. This tendency is called heterosexuality. Heterosexual attraction is part of God's plan to prepare men and women to marry and have children. As time passes, some of your attractions may result in good friendships with persons of the other gender, and one attraction may eventually lead to marriage.

Some people continue to be attracted primarily to those of the same gender. This tendency is called homosexuality. The Church teaches that two people of the same gender may not express affection in ways that are appropriate for married love only. One of the reasons for this is that their physical relationship cannot be open to new life.

Attraction between the genders is often the first step in falling in love. But because the basis for good relationships is who you are, not how you look, physical appearance is only one source of attraction. A woman and man may be attracted to each other spiritually because they share religious beliefs and moral values. They may have an emotional attraction to each other's temperament or personality. Or one person may find another's intellectual gifts attractive.

Feeling attraction is part of being human. It happens to people in all vocations. We have the ability to determine how we will respond to these natural feelings of attraction. We are called to exercise self-control and show self-respect and respect for others. Within marriage the **sexual desire**, or longing, that a husband and wife have for each other can be expressed in chaste, loving, faithful, and intimate ways. When sexual desire is misused, it becomes **lust**.

Loving
like Jesus

Jesus' life, death, and resurrection redeemed us, or saved us, from the power of sin and everlasting death and gave us hope to be with God forever.

To love as Jesus did is to show a saving love that reaches out to touch people's lives and make them better. Throughout time Christians have loved as Jesus did. As you read some of their stories, think about ways you can reach out and show love to the people in your own life.

Love in Action

Mother Teresa loved those whom others ignored. She bathed and fed poor people who were dying in filth in the streets of India. She gave them homes where they could die with dignity. In each person, Mother Teresa said, she saw the face of Jesus.

Cesar Chavez gave hope to migrant farm workers, the poorest laborers in the United States. Unjust landowners made huge profits but did not pay their workers enough for them to live healthy lives. Chavez organized the laborers into a union that worked for fair pay and better living conditions.

Harriet Tubman's people called her Moses because she led slaves to places where they would be free. Risking her own life, Tubman helped more than 1,000 African Americans escape from slavery.

Nicholas of Myra led a life of generous giving. He enjoyed secretly leaving gifts for those in need. People today know him as Saint Nicholas, the inspiration for the giving of gifts at Christmas.

To love as Jesus did, try to see each person as he would. A friend of yours may be sick with chicken pox or the flu or may even have a life-threatening illness. Some classmates may feel left out because they don't have what's in fashion. Some are called names and are not invited to join in activities. What can you do for them? To act in a just way, what could you say to a person who is picking on someone else?

Keeping in Touch

When you're sorting out your feelings for someone you like, try spending some quiet time with God in prayer.

Find a quiet place with no distractions. Breathe slowly, in and out, several times. Think of a name for God that you like. Say this name over and over in the quiet of your heart.

If your mind is busy thinking, concentrate on the fact that God loves you, just as you are. Enjoy God being with you.

Then write a short letter to God about your feelings.

Hi, God! It's me, _____

I feel _____

_____

_____

_____

_____

_____

HomeLink For Your Family

We shared this chapter. _____
We have these questions or comments:

_____

_____

_____

I have called you by name:
you are mine.
You are precious in my eyes
and glorious,
and I love you.

(based on Isaiah 43:1, 4)

Prayers and Resources

The Sign of the Cross

In the name of the Father,
and of the Son,
and of the Holy Spirit.
Amen.

The Lord's Prayer

Our Father, who art in heaven,
hallowed be thy name;
thy kingdom come;
thy will be done on earth as it is in heaven.
Give us this day our daily bread;
and forgive us our trespasses
as we forgive those who trespass against us;
and lead us not into temptation.
but deliver us from evil.
Amen.

Hail Mary

Hail, Mary, full of grace,
the Lord is with you!
Blessed are you among women,
and blessed is the fruit of your womb, Jesus.
Holy Mary, Mother of God,
pray for us sinners,
now and at the hour of our death.
Amen.

Glory to the Father (Doxology)

Glory to the Father, and to the Son, and to the
  Holy Spirit:
as it was in the beginning, is now, and will be
  for ever.
Amen.

Blessing Before Meals

Bless us, O Lord, and these your gifts
which we are about to receive from your goodness.
Through Christ our Lord.
Amen.

Thanksgiving After Meals

We give you thanks for all your gifts, almighty God,
living and reigning now and for ever.
Amen.

A Family Prayer

Lord our God, bless this household.
May we be blessed with health, goodness of heart,
gentleness, and the keeping of your law.
We give thanks to you,
Father, Son, and Holy Spirit,
now and for ever.
Amen.

The Great Commandment

"You shall love the Lord, your God, with all your
heart, with all your being, with all your strength,
and with all your mind, and your neighbor as
yourself."
(Luke 10:27)

Prayer to the Holy Spirit

Come, Holy Spirit, fill the hearts of your faithful.
And kindle in them the fire of your love.
Send forth your Spirit and they shall be created.
And you will renew the face of the earth.
Lord,
by the light of your Holy Spirit
you have taught the hearts of your faithful.
In that same Spirit
help us choose what is right
and always rejoice in your consolation.
We ask this through Christ our Lord.
Amen.

Act of Contrition

My God,
I am sorry for my sins with all my heart.
In choosing to do wrong
and failing to do good,
I have sinned against you
whom I should love above all things.
I firmly intend, with your help,
to do penance,
to sin no more,
and to avoid whatever leads me to sin.
Our Savior Jesus Christ
suffered and died for us.
In his name, my God, have mercy.

The Jesus Prayer

Lord Jesus Christ,
Son of God,
have mercy on me, a sinner.
Amen.

The Beatitudes

Blessed are the poor in spirit,
  for theirs is the kingdom of heaven.
Blessed are they who mourn,
  for they will be comforted.
Blessed are the meek,
  for they will inherit the land.
Blessed are they who hunger and thirst for
    righteousness,
  for they will be satisfied.
Blessed are the merciful,
  for they will be shown mercy.
Blessed are the clean of heart,
  for they will see God.
Blessed are the peacemakers,
  for they will be called children of God.
Blessed are they who are persecuted for the sake
    of righteousness,
  for theirs is the kingdom of heaven.
(Matthew 5:3–10)

The Ten Commandments

1. I am the Lord your God. You shall not have strange gods before me.
2. You shall not take the name of the Lord your God in vain.
3. Remember to keep holy the Lord's day.
4. Honor your father and your mother.
5. You shall not kill.
6. You shall not commit adultery.
7. You shall not steal.
8. You shall not bear false witness against your neighbor.
9. You shall not covet your neighbor's wife.
10. You shall not covet your neighbor's goods.

Works of Mercy

Corporal (for the body)	Spiritual (for the spirit)
Feed the hungry.	Warn the sinner.
Give drink to the thirsty.	Teach the ignorant.
Clothe the naked.	Counsel the doubtful.
Shelter the homeless.	Comfort the sorrowful.
Visit the sick.	Bear wrongs patiently.
Visit the imprisoned.	Forgive injuries.
Bury the dead.	Pray for the living and the dead.

Gifts of the Holy Spirit

Wisdom
Understanding
Right judgment (Counsel)
Courage (Fortitude)
Knowledge
Reverence (Piety)
Wonder and awe (Fear of the Lord)

Fruits of the Spirit

Charity	Generosity
Joy	Gentleness
Peace	Faithfulness
Patience	Modesty
Kindness	Self-control
Goodness	Chastity

Virtues

Theological	Cardinal
Faith	Prudence
Hope	Justice
Love	Fortitude
	Temperance